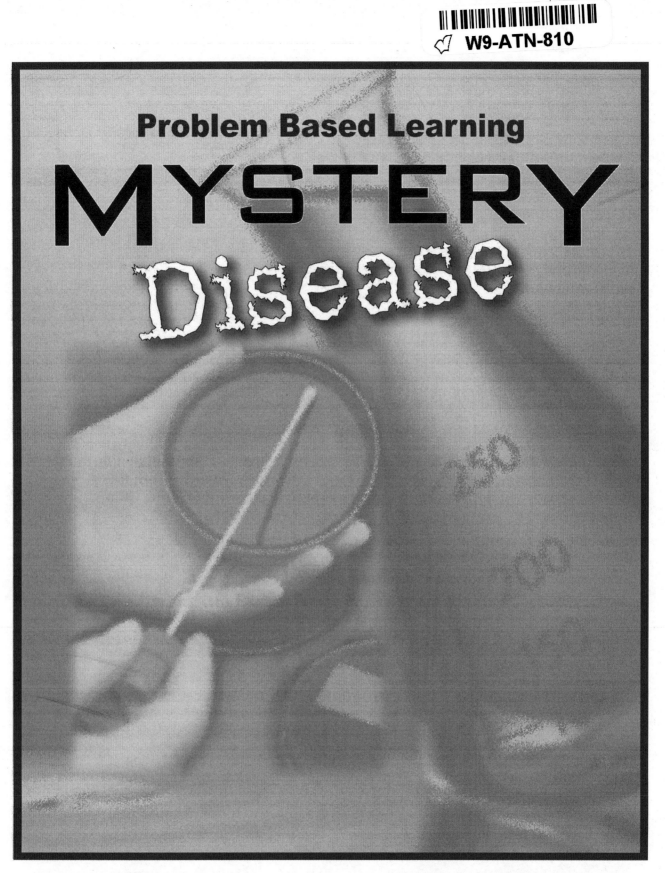

**Problem Based Learning**

# MYSTERY
## Disease

Written by: **Mark A. Bohland**  Illustrated by: **Stephanie O'Shaughnessy**

Edited by Dianne Draze and Sonsie Conroy
Published by Prufrock Press Inc.

ISBN-13: 978-1-59363-110-9
ISBN-10: 1-59363-110-3

Questions regarding this book should be addressed to:
**Prufrock Press Inc.**
P.O. Box 8813
Waco, TX 76714-8813
800-998-2208

For more information about Prufrock Press products, visit our website
**www.prufrock.com**

# Contents

# Acknowledgments

I would like to acknowledge the following people for their help and support in writing this book:

☆ My wife, who knows the difference between "there" and "their," which my spell checker does not, and who allows me the time to leisurely get lost in learning and lesson planning.

☆ My students, who found misspellings that even my wife missed, who asked hard questions and who pointed out some possible inconsistencies and areas of confusion in the earliest drafts of this unit.

☆ Our school nurse, our public health nurses and especially our county sanitarian, without whom this unit would not exist in its current form.

☆ Mrs. Beach, my mentor, an accomplished teacher who expects excellence and gets it from her students. She is willing to help other teachers become and achieve the same.

# Introduction

## Why Problem Based Learning?

Whether teaching students who have been officially identified as gifted, or working with any bright students, teachers are often confronted with the dilemma of concentrating on content or process. This is especially true when the teacher has a limited amount of time to work with students. Some teachers opt for an emphasis on extending the depth or breadth of the curriculum. Others focus on activities designed to promote higher-level thinking skills, activities that in many cases may be viewed as merely fun and games with little correlation to the curriculum.

A problem based learning (PBL) unit is specifically designed for student-centered learning of new and meaningful content in a way that forces students to grapple with a complex and changing problem, requiring higher level thinking skills, in an environment where students work both individually and in collaboration with others.

## A Mystery Disease

The scenario for this unit takes place in early September. The fair has just ended and school has begun. What would normally be a time of getting back to routine becomes a time of panic. A disease begins sweeping though the small community of Jamestown. As people show up at the hospital it becomes the responsibility of county health department staff to determine what the disease is and to find its source. Is it one of the food vendors at the fair? Is it from the animals at the fair? Can it be traced to one of the surrounding farms? As country health staff, students have to examine all the evidence, make recommendations to save the lives of the people who have contracted the disease, determine the most probable source, and make recommendations to make sure this will not happen again.

This open-ended assignment will draw students into a real-life drama. From day to day and even hour to hour they will be making decisions that affect peoples' lives. The motivation is built in.

## Teacher's Role

Good teachers enjoy teaching. However, teacher-led instruction isn't always best for students. In a PBL unit, teachers "teach" very little, while students learn to solve problems and research new information. Students also learn to process the content both individually and as part of a group whose members have various priorities and world views. In a PBL unit, the classroom teacher becomes a facilitator of student-led learning.

## What Students Do

The curriculum in a PBL unit is not merely "more of the same." Students may explore the depth and breadth of a topic, but that is not all they do. Once information has been acquired, it is used in complex and practical ways. Just as in real-world situations, things change as students work toward a solution, forcing students to rethink assumptions and conclusions, as well as requiring them to discover new information.

Students must evaluate competing ideas and values as they grapple with a problem that does not have one clear-cut solution. As students develop a plan of action to solve their problem, it becomes quite evident that there may be several different yet valid solutions. Students, who may be naturally opinionated and may typically be strong leaders, now find themselves in a group of like-minded individuals who must agree on a plan of action.

All of this learning takes place in the context of a real-world problem, which itself makes learning more meaningful and interesting to many of these students. Teachers will find a PBL unit to be a refreshing and exciting way to facilitate learning among bright and gifted students. A PBL unit maximizes the use of limited time, allowing for both content acquisition and process development skills, in a way that is both exciting and challenging for the students.

Kathy Goodwin
490 Roberts Rd.
Athens, GA 30606

**Make Adaptations**

This unit was originally designed for intermediate through junior high academically talented students in a full-day pullout program that met once a week. It could just as easily (and maybe more easily) be used in a class that meets every day. You may have to make changes to adapt the unit to your classroom situation. Review the materials and decide how you will integrate the unit into your schedule. You may want to add an extra day or two between sessions to allow students time to complete their reports. The unit can be adapted to several different time lines. Read through the introductory material and plan the schedule for your unit before you begin.

**Using the Internet**

The unit assumes students have Internet access in the classroom. While this unit is not a mere web-quest, it makes extensive use of Internet resources. The unit can be used without student access to the Internet if you are willing to provide copies of pertinent information that you have found through your research or which is available from your local health department.

Students may need a bit of a push in the right direction when doing Internet research. Start with search engines like www.excite.com, www.google.com, or www.altavista.com, for this type of search. Students should be able to suggest search terms from their common information. A search of the terms "stomach cramps," "diarrhea," "bloody diarrhea" and "fever" should provide plenty of background information for the students. If they need additional help, the combination, "stomach cramps and bloody diarrhea" should give them all they need.

**Allocate Time**

The unit is designed to be completed in nine to eleven sessions plus an introduction to problem based learning. The introduction and session 1 can be combined if you have a large enough block of time.

Typically you will need about two hours for each of the sessions. Actual judged presentations take about 10 minutes per group, with an additional 5 minutes per group for the judges to tabulate the scores.

The simulation covers nine crisis days. The days of the crisis will not necessarily correspond to nine classroom days. Depending on the amount of time you meet with your class, the work for some crisis days can be accomplished in one classroom period. For other crisis days, it will take a couple of class meetings to complete the simulation.

The first day of the crisis is on September 6 (this can be any date in your real schedule). This day is session 2 in your lesson plan. The crisis calendar ends on September 13. The directions for all sessions relate to a day of the crisis. This could be any day in your class schedule.

**Preview Unit**

You will play the role of Dr. Billman, the chief of staff of the county health department. In this role, you will have to be familiar with each day's activities, distribute information to students, and guide students' work. Make sure to familiarize yourself with the material for all sessions of the unit before introducing any of the material. This will give you a feel for the flow of the unit from day to day.

**Select Judges**

You will need three judges to evaluate students' final presentations. People who have a background in public health, sanitation or medicine, or local government make good judges. Explain how much time they will be expected to devote to the evaluations. Schedule a date for the presentations that is acceptable to all judges. You may want to have a back-up judge in case one of the judges has to drop out at the last minute.

Make copies of all materials for each judge and give them the materials well in advance of the presentation day so they have plenty of time to become familiar with the problem.

**Group Students**

Determine optimal student groupings for your class. Four to five students per group is ideal. Consider whether you will have groups composed of students who have demonstrated leadership in the past, groups composed of followers, or whether you want groups composed of a mixture of leaders and followers. Also think about whether you want mixed grade level groups or single grade level groups. Choose the grouping that will be best for your students.

Assign or have each group choose a team leader.

**Crisis Calendar**

| class session | simulated day | simulated date | |
|---|---|---|---|
| 1 | 1 | Wed., Sept 5 | |
| 2 | 2 | Thurs, Sept. 6 | |
| 3 | 3 | Fri., Sept. 7 | |
| 4 | 4 & 5 | Sat. & Sun., Sept. 8 & 9 | no work on Sunday, day 5 |
| 5 | 6 | Mon., Sept. 10 | |
| 6 | 7 | Tues., Sept. 11 | |
| 7 | 8 | Wed., Sept. 12 | review and develop presentations |
| 8 | 9 | early on Thurs., Sept. 13 | practice presentations with teacher<br>town meeting (optional)<br>continue working on presentations |
| 9 | | | practice presentations with teacher, finish presentations |
| 10 | 9 | later on Thurs., Sept. 13 | final presentations to judges |

**Introduce PBL**

Before you begin, take some time to introduce problem based learning to your students. Using the information in the letter to parents (page 24-25) as a guide, discuss how PBL units differ from other, more structured assignments. Go through the example of the flooded baseball field. Tell them that their assignment will be like the third assignment, somewhat vague and open to interpretation.

Point out that they will be working in groups to solve the problem. How they respond to information they receive during the simulation will determine what kind of information they receive in the future. Therefore, two teams may come up with two entirely different solutions. At the end of the project they will present their findings to a team of judges.

Explain that they will receive information in several different ways. They will receive directions from Dr. Billman, the chief doctor of the county public health department. They will receive copies of contagious disease reports from the hospital. They will also discover information on their own by using the Internet or other resources.

Encourage them to continue working with their team even when they feel frustrated. Tell them that their success is dependent on their ability to be resourceful, work as a team, and continue to work even when they are frustrated by the ambiguity of the situation.

**Parents' Guide**

Ask students to give their parents copies of the information and discuss the unit with them. Instruct them to have their parents sign the permission slips and return them.

**Explain Roles**

The students' first roles will be as emergency room nurses. They should be able to make a tentative diagnosis of E. coli-based food poisoning in 1½ to 3 hours. Since there are several illnesses with similar symptoms, students should be cautioned not to be too quick to settle on a final diagnosis.

Students may respond surprisingly well if they are told ahead of time that they will, just like real nurses, be dealing with illnesses and unpleasant bodily functions; and that they will have the opportunity to demonstrate their maturity by the way they discuss things like vomiting and diarrhea without crudeness or giggling.

After this first session, they will assume the roles of employees of the country health department. Most of their information about the crisis will come from memos from Dr. Billman and contagious disease reports. They have to do independent research to get the additional information they need to successfully complete their assignments.

**Fuzzy Challenge**

Pass out copies of Fuzzy Challenge Procedures (handout 1.1, page 30). The process that is outlined on this sheet describes how teams can tackle a problem and work toward a satisfactory solution. Discuss the steps as they are outlined on the handout.

**Problem Overview**

Distribute copies of handout 1.2 (pages 31-32) and as a group read through the text. Give students a due date for the first part of the challenge, which is diagnosing the disease.

**Clues to the Diagnosis**

A clue is in the fifth paragraph of the students' common information. "Only one mother mentioned that her daughter had a fever; however, all parents mentioned severe stomach cramps and diarrhea. Some mentioned vomiting." Another key is in the ninth paragraph. "The other child, however, was still in the emergency room. Her stomach cramps were severe, and her diarrhea was bloody. The nursing staff was beginning to think it should have treated the first two patients differently and was wondering if it was about to see some kind of an epidemic." (anti-diarrheal agents are contraindicated for E. coli.)

**Chart**

The chart on page 10 will be helpful in guiding students toward a diagnosis that Dr. Billman can accept. This chart is for your use and is **not intended to be duplicated and distributed to students.** You can, however, use it to answer their questions and guide their research.

A positive identification of E. coli requires the testing of a stool sample and it may take 2 to 3 weeks to get results back from the lab. Once a tentative diagnosis of E. coli has been made, Dr. Billman will instruct the county health inspectors to proceed on the assumption that this is indeed an E. coli outbreak. You will, of course, never hear differently in the week and a half of the simulation calendar.

**Diagnosis**

Before session 2 students should have made the diagnosis of E. coli. This will be verified by the first communication from Dr. Billman in session 2.

9

# Chart of Symptoms

| Symptoms | stomach cramps | diarrhea | bloody diarrhea | fever | nausea and vomiting | chills | headache |
|---|---|---|---|---|---|---|---|
| present in this simulation | yes | yes | yes | only in one case | no | no | no |
| E. coli | yes | yes | yes | low grade or none | occasional | no | no |
| salmonella | yes | yes | occasional | yes | yes | yes | yes |
| shigella | yes | yes | yes | yes | yes | no | no |
| staphylococcus aureus | stomach pain | yes | no | yes | yes | yes | yes |

For instructor use. Do not duplicate and distribute to students.

**Make Diagnosis**

Before beginning session 2 all groups should have made an initial diagnosis of E. coli.

**Make Assignments**

Students will be presented with their assignments as county health inspectors, as outlined in "Doctor Billman's" first memo.

Students should be reminded that their final evaluation will be based upon how well they complete tasks one and two in Dr. Billman's first memo.

**Memo**

Pass out and discuss Dr. Billman's memo, handout 2.1 (page 33-34). Note when assignments will be due.

Explain to students that even though Dr. Billman instructs his staff to interview all victims and their families, they will not be doing any actual interviews. They will receive contagious disease reports on which information from the interviews has been recorded. Their jobs will be to analyze and interpret data on these reports.

Should you decide that you want students to do the third task, an informative presentation to a younger class, assign grades or classes for each group so they can make an age-appropriate presentation.

**Newspaper Articles**

Pass out handouts 2.2 and 2.3 (pages 35-36). Discuss the newspaper articles. Emphasize again, that what students will be doing in class is very similar to what people do on a daily basis in county health departments throughout the country.

**CDR I - 6**

Have students meet in their problem solving groups. Once students are in their small groups, pass out the first six contagious disease reports (handouts 2.4 - 2.9, pages 37 to 48). Remind the students that much of the information they will need to complete Dr. Billman's two tasks will be found in the CDRs. Give them time to read through the reports.

**Give Direction**

At this point students may seem to have endless questions or instant answers. However, this is a time for students to learn on their own. Comments and questions such as the following may be more helpful to the students in the long run, than the direct answers students may be hoping to get. Say things like:

✓ That's an interesting observation. Are you certain?
✓ What do you think?
✓ Where do you think you could find out?
✓ What makes you think that?

Younger students may need more guidance than older students, but neither should be spoon-fed the answers.

**Games**

Students may question what each game is like so they can decide if the games are potential sources of contamination. If they ask, you can tell them the games are as follows:

✓ duck pond - (sponsored by the band boosters) catch a rubber duck to win a prize

✓ basketball - shoot foul shots and win a prize

✓ ping pong/goldfish - (sponsored by the Methodist Church) throw a ping pong ball into a fish bowl and win a goldfish

✓ ring the bell - hit a lever with a hammer and make a steel ball go up and ring a bell and win a prize

**Food Booths**

Should students raise questions about the food that is referenced in the contagious disease reports you can give them this information:

✓ The Dairy Council sponsored the booth serving homemade ice cream

✓ The FFA (Future Farmers of America) served the hamburgers

✓ Elephant ears are pastries that are deep fried, brushed with butter, coated with cinnamon and sugar and served warm.

**Memo**

Pass out and discuss Dr. Billman's memo for session 3, handout 3.1 (page 49).

**Newspaper Articles**

Pass out the newspaper article, handout 3.2 (page 50) and let groups incorporate the information in this article into their research base.

**Map and Disease Reports**

Pass out the map of the fairgrounds (handout 3.3, page 51) and the next four contagious disease reports, handouts 3.4 to 3.7 (pages 52 to 59).

**Analyze Information**

Students may begin to see patterns or they may begin to try to force patterns that do not necessarily exist. Some groups may want to put an inflexible grasp on one possible source of E. coli and then try to construct a mythical chain connecting all other characters to that one source. You may hear something similar to, "Well character so-and-so got it from X and then maybe they touched a ketchup bottle at the hamburger stand and then so-and-so touched the ketchup bottle and then..."

Questions such as, "Are you certain?" and "What evidence do you have from the data to support your theory?" may be very helpful here.

Encourage students to develop tentative theories, but to be willing to modify those theories as new evidence is presented. Remind them that they have only seen about half of the contagious disease reports at this point.

You will want to emphasize that they will need to know more than just the minimal amount of information that is necessary to complete tasks one and two. Dr. Billman may have additional questions about complications and disease transmission that are not specifically addressed in tasks one and two. They need to accumulate any information that might be potentially important to the crisis. This sort of direction is designed in part to keep students from a tunnel vision approach to the tasks, as well as to prepare them to make life-saving decisions for two of the victims.

**Note**

One victim will die from complications known as hemolytic-uremic syndrome (HUS). This is not a result of the action or inaction of the student groups. Two other victims will exhibit similar symptoms and may or may not be saved by some of your groups, depending on the groups' actions.

By now some overly eager or less thorough groups may have identified everything from undercooked French fries to a visit from the dairy council president as a cause of the E. coli outbreak. Students may need to be encouraged to predict the "most likely" sources of contamination and methods of transmission for the disease. Some of the data on the contagious disease reports, (especially on page 2 of each report) is unnecessary information. Some is potentially misleading.

**Memo and CDRs**

Distribute Dr. Billman's memo, handout 4.1 (page 60) and the next three contagious disease reports, handouts 4.2 to 4.4 (pages 61 to 66). Give students time to integrate the new information.

**Responses to Dr. Billman**

Beginning with Session 5, students will be informed that their responses to Dr. Billman will have an effect on his responses to them and also to the outcome of the crisis. Beginning with the start of session 7, there will be different memos from Dr. Billman depending on what memos the groups have sent to him.

You need to be aware of the possibility that a group may want to correspond with Dr. Billman to make a general suggestion, which might better be incorporated into their final report. For instance, students may run up to the teacher's desk with every possible scenario and ask, "Is this right?" They should be encouraged to carefully analyze the data and to present their conclusions and recommendations to Dr. Billman on the appointed day.

On the other hand, now is the time to begin hinting that students will want to immediately provide Dr. Billman with a memo from their group, if they determine that anybody is in immediate danger or if there is something that needs to be done right away. Three students are in danger of developing HUS. It is rare that any group will act in time to save Susie Thompson. This is by design. Prompt and correct action can, however, easily save the lives of Anthony Green and Darryl Harper. Make sure groups have a mechanism for getting vital information to Dr. Billman.

Remind students that the fair is already over for this year, but suggestions for next year should be presented in their final report.

**Your Role**

You will, of course, want to assist students as needed. However, the emphasis should be on encouraging students to begin to develop research, reasoning, and leadership skills that will enable them to work through real-world problems on their own.

This may be the most critical day of the unit for many groups. Things change rapidly at this point. Many groups who thought their research was over will find themselves retracing their efforts, looking for new clues in old data as well as doing new research.

**Memos**

Students will also receive three formal communications from Dr. Billman today (handouts 5.1, 5.6, and 5.7). Assuming a full day pullout program, the first memo (5.1, page 67) should be handed out at the beginning of the class, before the contagious disease reports. The second communication (5.6, page 76) could be handed out at about the middle of the day, and the third one (5.7, page 77) about a half hour or so before class is to be dismissed for the day. If you do not have a full-day program, plan the distribution of Dr. Billman's memos to allow students enough time between communications to take appropriate action.

**Disease Reports**

Students will receive the last four contagious disease reports (handouts 5.2 - 5.5, pages 68 - 75) today. There is no report for Mrs. Pataky, a 68-year-old female (from the first wave of patients at the emergency room), because she is on vacation and no one has been able to contact her.

Mention to students that this in an interactive unit and their responses will make a difference in what happens in the unit and what information they receive in the future. Depending on their communications with Dr. Billman, different groups will affect the outcome of this crisis in different ways.

**Responses to Save Lives**

In order to save Anthony Green's life, a group must communicate with Dr. Billman in writing that Anthony is exhibiting symptoms of HUS and should be transferred to a hospital specializing in the treatment of acute kidney disease as soon as possible. To save Anthony's life, this communication must be received prior to the start of session 7.

Students may ask where such a hospital exists, and with some simple logic or research, they should conclude a large city such as "Capitol City," or other city appropriate to your situation.

On page 2 of Darryl Harper's contagious disease report, students should note that he too has developed a rash. Even though the clue for Darryl is presented prior to the one for Anthony, it is not as obvious, and groups have until the start of session 8 to save his life in the same manner as noted above for Anthony.

**Students' Work**

Students will spend the session reevaluating the data, researching HUS, writing a public letter, developing conclusions, and considering possible plans of action.

**Memos and Maps**

Pass out memo 6.1 (page 78) and the two maps (handouts 6.2 and 6.3, pages 79 - 80) at the beginning of the session.

Encourage students to develop a system of organization for their data and to concentrate on what they can suggest from the data, not what they think might have happened.

**Memo**

Pass out memo 6.4 (page 81), about half to three-fourths of the way through the session.

**Letter to Newspaper**

During this session groups should hand in their letters to the public that will be printed in the newspaper.

**Communications with Dr. Billman**

Remind students of how they can communicate with Dr. Billman. They can send their comments via handwritten notes or typed memos that are placed in a box you have designated for these communications. They could also communicate via e-mail to you. Stress that communication to Dr. Billman must be based on the data and on students' research. Some student groups should be making a diagnosis of HUS for Darryl Harper and Anthony Green and sending you recommendations for their treatment.

**Memo**

Pass out one of two memos from Dr. Billman (handout 7.1 on page 82 or handout 7.2 on page 83) at the beginning of the session. Which memo students receive will depend on whether they properly diagnosed Anthony's illness and recommended that he be transferred to a hospital that could treat HUS. Use handout 7.1 for groups who did not respond to save Anthony's life. Use handout 7.2 for groups who were able to save his life.

**Editorials**

Distribute handouts 7.3 and 7.4 (pages 84-86). These are copies of an editorial and letters to the editor that were referred to earlier in memos from Dr. Billman. The opinions offered should be considered when students make recommendations for future community activities (like the fair) or the community's response to health crises.

**Meet with Leaders**

Meet with group leaders individually to assess their group's progress on:

✓ Determining a probable cause or causes of the outbreak
✓ Developing an action plan for next year's fair
✓ Discovering who may be at special risk and what to do to save their lives
✓ Planning a presentation for the lower elementary children.

**Group Work**

Group leaders should prioritize activities and consider delegating separate responsibilities to group members to maximize the use of time.

This may be one of the more pressure-filled days for the groups, as they begin to realize that final presentations are not far off, that they have received as much data as is going to be available, and that there are still no clear-cut answers.

Encourage groups to find ways to combine their individual research and reasoning efforts into a unified whole. Expect personality clashes. This is a real-world simulation, and this is the day that things tend to get "real."

**Memos**

Memos (handout 8.1 or 8.2, pages 87-88) regarding Darryl Harper should be passed out at the beginning of the session. Which memo students receive depends on whether they diagnosed Darryl's HUS and took appropriate action. Distribute handout 8.1 to those groups who were able to respond to save Daryl's life. Give handout 8.2 to those groups who were not able to make recommendations to that would save Daryl's life.

**Practice
Presentations**

Students need a chance to practice in front of the teacher prior to making their final presentations. You should ask difficult questions, simulating what a judge might ask. You may want to ask probing questions regarding their thought processes, their logical jumps and conclusions, their understanding of the simulation scenario, and their understanding of the scientific content and sociological implications upon which the scenario is based. Their responses should provide you with a list of questions to share with the judges.

After doing a practice presentation, many groups suddenly realize how much more preparation they need before presenting to a panel of real doctors and nurses. Some things to suggest to the groups that might help them improve their presentations are:
- ✓ Tell what you can reasonably infer from the data. Don't make up things.
- ✓ Share duties. Different group members can make different parts of the presentation.
- ✓ Use visual aids.
- ✓ Be prepared to answer questions about related information.

**Work on
Presentations**

Give students the rest of the time to refine their presentations. Students should be encouraged to bring any necessary art materials they need for making visual aids.

## Session 9

**Dress Rehearsal**

Students will practice making their presentations to you for the last time. Again, ask challenging questions.

They will then make final modifications to their final presentations for the panel of judges.

**Why a Town Meeting?**
The town forum is an activity that accomplishes several goals. It gives the students a mental break from research, which is important for those students have not previously spent this much time researching information without a specific road map to guide their research. Other students may be having disagreements with group members regarding the "correct" answer to the problem and need a break from each other. The town forum also gives students an opportunity to express what they have been learning without giving away their group's secrets. Most importantly, the town forum will allow students to begin to understand and appreciate the problem from other perspectives.

**Guidelines**
The town meeting, moderated by the editor of the *Barrow County Sentinel*, is a panel discussion, where citizens, represented by those who wrote letters to the editor, express their positions. Some students will be assigned specific roles, while others are concerned citizens or audience members. The moderator can ask a question and let each panelist answer it "in character." After three or four questions the moderator may open the floor to questions from the community.

**Choose Roles**
Choose your moderator carefully. A strong but fair-minded person is needed to make this discussion work. You will also want to carefully choose the person to play Mr. Black, the belligerent outsider who has moved to this traditional rural community. Choose the forum participants carefully and coach them on their point of view and demeanor:

| person | role/point of view | demeanor |
|---|---|---|
| moderator **John Brandon** | editor of the *Sentinel* He must stay neutral and make sure everyone gets a chance to be heard. | conciliatory |
| **Pat Yoder** | president, Barrow County Dairy Council | reassuring |
| **Claudius Black** | concerned citizen He must be a good actor. | belligerent, antagonistic |
| **Alex Workman** | FFA secretary/treasurer | defensive |
| **Stacy Heilman** | county fair board president | politically cautious |

Other panel members can be added as your situation suggests. It is best not to have more than five or six panel members plus the moderator.

**Session 10**

**Final
Presentations**

Students will make final presentations to the three judges. Their presentations should cover the following points:

✓ Identify the most probable source of the E. coli outbreak, defending their theory with research and solid logic.

✓ Present a plan to deal with similar situations in the future. This plan should address all possible sources of the disease that may have been responsible for the recent outbreak.

Student groups should present separately, and groups should be kept in a separate room until it is their turn to present. Since the students will want to see each other's presentations, videotaping may be advisable. This also gives less diligent groups a chance to see what can be done with appropriate effort.

**Questions**

Judges should be given a list of possible questions — four or five easy and four or five probing questions. Ideally, each judge will ask one or two questions of each group after that group's presentation. Encourage judges to ask probing questions.

**Timing**

Most presentations, including the question-and-answer period with the judges, will last from 10 to 15 minutes, depending on the grade level of the group.

Judges should be allowed about five minutes to fill out the evaluation sheets.

**Results**

After all groups have presented, scores may be tallied and awards presented to the top team. If you have videotaped the presentations, you can let students view the videotape.

# Evaluation and Debriefing

**Evaluation Forms**
Students and the teacher should complete the evaluation forms (pages 28 and 29). This may be done separately followed by a teacher-student conference or the teacher may do the evaluation during the conference.

Students should be reminded to evaluate both their performance and their effort. While it is important to recognize the diligence and hard work of low-performing students, it is also important to encourage significant effort toward excellence in students whose minimal efforts result in the best work in the class.

**Student Input**
Students may wish to share their ideas regarding the overall unit. Some may have suggestions for improving the unit for the next time you use it or for another PBL unit. This unit, as presented, is in several ways different from the way it was originally presented, thanks to student input.

**Thank Yous**
This would also be a good time to have students write thank you cards for the judges, speakers, and any others who have not already been formally thanked.

**Presentations to Younger Classes**
Students may work on their presentation to younger elementary school students. Previous groups have created songs, coloring pages, games and even a one-act play to communicate the importance of cleanliness and food preparation and storage safety to younger children.

## The "Right" Answers

Problem base learning, by definition, deals with situations that lend themselves to more than one possible solution. This is especially true for the final plan that a group might present in this simulation. However, as students work through the problem, it may be helpful for you to understand some of the clues built into the unit, as well as some of the false leads that have been created. This may help you to keep students from over-committing to a direction that will ultimately prove frustrating.

This information is for your use and is not intended to be duplicated and distributed to students. With that in mind:

✓ In the chart of common symptoms, E. coli most closely matches the presenting symptoms.

✓ No evidence exists to suggest that anything at the Baptist Church camp caused the illness.

✓ Mothers know when something is wrong with their children, but they often don't know why.

✓ Charlie tended goats and swam in a pond that may have received runoff from a cow pasture on the neighboring Johnson farm.

✓ David Jones not only came into contact with Allen Johnson but may have had contact with several of the infected children.

✓ Allen Johnson demonstrates obsessive-compulsive behavior. While hand washing is not specifically mentioned, other children tease him about his cleanliness. If E. coli bacteria were present on his farm, this behavior might suggest why he is not ill.

✓ LuAnne Brown may have simply done what many children do. She ate everything available at the fair and got an upset stomach.

✓ Mary Smith and Mr. McCoy ate unwashed tomatoes from his garden. Manure for that garden came from the Johnson Farm. Neither Mary nor her grandmother ate vegetables at the new restaurant, The Garden Spot.

✓ Did Mr. Black and his daughter become ill from just walking through the fair or was the best new restaurant in town not so special after all?

✓ Many students become concerned when the elderly lady from the first day at the emergency room cannot be located. Apparently, she is on vacation.

✓ Three students are in danger of developing HUS. It is rare that any group will act in time to save Susie Thompson. This is by design. Prompt and correct action can, however, easily save the other two lives.

✓ Deep frying food would kill E. coli bacteria.

✓ E coli is spread primarily by eating undercooked beef products or contact with feces from ruminates (cows, sheep, goats, deer, but not ponies) either directly or by eating fruits and vegetables that have been in contact with such feces and have not been properly washed.

# Other Teacher Resources

Incorporating community resources into your PBL unit adds a degree of realism. Local resources fall into three broad categories:

## Research Sources

- librarians
- medical schools
- health care professionals
- high school students involved in FFA
- field trips
- farms
- restaurants
- fair food vendors (There may be vendors in your community who may even bring a food trailer to your school for a day.)
- food service classes at your high school or the vocational school
- health care facilities
- county health offices
- laboratories and other testing facilities
- doctors
- nurses
- county health inspectors

## Internet Resources *

Problem Based Learning

    http://www.imsa.edu/team/cpbl/cpbl.html

    http://www.pbli.org/

E. coli

    http://cincinnati.com/nie/archive/09-14-99/

    http://people.ku.edu/%7Ejbrown/ecoli.html

    http://www.cdc.gov/ncidod/dbmd/diseaseinfo/escherichiacoli_g.htm

    http://www.about-ecoli.com/

    http://vm.cfsan.fda.gov/~mow/chap15.html

    http://www.indoorpurifiers.com/ozonefood.htm

* Links above were active at the time of publication.

## Newspaper Articles

Newspaper articles in this unit, while based on actual events, are fictional. An Internet search using the term "E. coli" and "county fair" will return links to several actual newspaper articles. If you use actual articles, from the Internet or from your local newspaper, make sure not to use articles that include information regarding specific causes (other than contaminated food) or editorial comment regarding plans or suggestions to decrease the chance of infection.

Parents' Introduction

to

# Problem Based Learning

We are about to begin a new unit, and this letter is to let you know what kind of new learning adventure your child will be experiencing. The unit is a problem based learning unit. It promises to be both exciting and challenging.

It will not be challenging because of the actual difficulty of the assignment, but because students may have never participated in this type of learning exercise before. This particular unit will offer students the opportunity to learn about contagious diseases, biohazards, public health, disease control, social science and systems, public speaking, and more. The unit will be a "fuzzy challenge," a more open-ended assignment than most students are used to.

## ✦ An example of problem based learning

Fuzzy challenges are designed to help students learn new information in a way that is very similar to real-world, adult-life situations. For example, if we had a flooded baseball field, I could give several assignments to my ball field committee, such as:

- Dig a ditch from the field to the creek and drain the field.
- Get the water off the field.
- Get the field ready for our Fourth of July picnic.

Each assignment is less specific and more fuzzy than the one before it. In the first one, the committee knows exactly what is expected. In the second assignment, the committee knows the goal, but they are free to accomplish it as they see fit. For the last assignment the committee knows that something needs to be accomplished, but they are not sure what that is. Do they get the field into playing condition for baseball or make sure it stays flooded and stock it with trout for a children's fishing contest?

In PBL much of the assignment is stated in fuzzy terms like the third assignment above. The students must first restate the problem to make sure they are headed in the right direction. They must then ask themselves what knowledge or skills are necessary to solve the problem and which of those things they currently lack.

If (in the previous example) they determine that the committee chairman wants a fishing derby, they will not be told to call Johnson's Fish Company, find out the cost of a dozen trout and then determine the total cost of 240 trout. That would be no more than a simple word problem combined with an exercise in telephone etiquette. In a PBL unit, on the other hand, they might be asked to present a report to the committee chairman, detailing their plans for utilizing the flooded ball field for a children's fishing derby. Students then would be divided into work teams and would present their competing plans on the final day of the unit.

**24**

### ✦ A mysterious disease

This year's fuzzy challenge, "Mystery Disease" is outlined in the information in your child's folder. Ask him or her to share the unit information with you and explain to you just what he or she currently doesn't know but needs to find out to complete the assignment. As the students work through this assessment phase and then find the information they need to complete the assignment, real self-directed learning is taking place.

Please don't let your child become overwhelmed or give up as they work on this problem. This type of unit will give students the skills that will stand them in good stead as they prepare to enter young adulthood. The work they do in this type of learning situation is very worthwhile.

This unit will require some out-of-class work, but it should be fun. Please allow your child to use the phone, the computer, or the public library as necessary.

While you are welcome to visit our classes any day, you are also invited to be present as the students make their final presentations. I know it would mean a great deal to your child if you could attend their presentation.

The unit involves realistic scenarios, including illness and death, which may upset some sensitive students. Therefore, I am requesting that parents sign a permission slip allowing their children to participate. Please sign the permission request, indicating whether or not your child is able to participate, and return it to me by _____.

As usual, I am available to speak with you individually regarding this unit or your child's and progress. My phone number is _____.

✂ · · · · · · · · · · · · · · · · · · · · · · · · · · · · · · · · · · · · · · · · · · · · · · · · · · · ·

# Parental Permission
### ✶ ✶ ✶ ✶
### Problem Based Learning Unit

Child's name _____

⭕ I give my permission for my child to participate in this unit.

⭕ I do not wish to have my child participate in this unit.

✎ _____

signature

_____

printed name

_____

date

Dear _____,

Thank you for agreeing to evaluate our students' presentations. Your participation adds another element of realism to this learning exercise.

I have enclosed a copy of all the materials given to parents and students. The section entitled "Parents' Introduction to Problem Based Learning" may be particularly helpful in explaining what our students will been doing during this unit. You do not necessarily need to read all of the contagious disease reports, but the student information sheets should enable you to get a feel for what is going on in the community. You will also want to be familiar with the maps of the county and of the fairgrounds.

Students will make presentations and then ask if you have any questions. Each judge should ask at least one question of each group. While we strive for and reward excellence, we do not wish to unnecessarily embarrass students whose presentations do not meet our expectations. Please try to ask questions that you feel are commensurate with the presentation you just heard. As you hear better presentations, please feel free to ask more difficult, probing questions. After any presentation, feel free to ask a question about anything you heard that is definitely in error. Judges may ask more than one question each.

You will rate each presentation on an evaluation form. Please use the entire range of points. Points should reflect both the ranking of groups and the comparative quality of their presentations.

Thank you again for your time and commitment to the education of our children.

Sincerely,

26

# Judges' Evaluation Form

Judge's name_____

Group _____

Assign points according to the following standards. Use the entire range of evaluation scores.

| | | | | |
|---|---|---|---|---|
| 10 | **outstanding** | 5 | | |
| 9 | | 4 | **poor** | |
| 8 | **very good** | 3 | | |
| 7 | | 2 | **inadequate** | |
| 6 | **average** | 1 | | |

✓ We would not expect the first and last place teams to have scores that are very similar.

✓ Each team should be asked at least one question by each judge.

✓ Please evaluate each of the following categories, based on the scale above.

| | judge's evaluation | weight of score | total score |
|---|---|---|---|
| • knowledge of E. coli: causes, symptoms, treatment, complications | _____ | x 2 | _____ /20 |
| • knowledge of the transmission of disease pathogens | _____ | x 2 | _____ /20 |
| • group analysis of the data | _____ | x 2 | _____ /20 |
| • student research skills as evidenced by their reference to source material | _____ | x 2 | _____ /20 |
| • the group action plan addresses all problems, is practical and creative | _____ | x 3 | _____ /30 |
| • organization of presentation | _____ | x 1 | _____ /10 |
| • public presentation skills | _____ | x 1 | _____ /10 |
| • relevance of any handouts, charts, etc. | _____ | x 1 | _____ /10 |
| • overall quality of the presentation | _____ | x 1 | _____ /10 |
| **total score** | | | _____ /150 |

**Rank** _____ **of** _____ **teams**

# Student Evaluation Form

Name _____

## Evaluation scale

| quality of work | | effort put into the project | |
|---|---|---|---|
| **1** | exceeded the expectations | **W** | did my best work possible |
| **2** | met most or all of the expectations | **X** | put forth very good effort |
| **3** | met some of the expectations | **Y** | did just enough work to get by |
| **4** | did not meet the expectations | **Z** | did not put in sufficient work |

Rate the quality of your work on this unit by assigning both a number (quality of work) and a letter (effort) for each of the following:

Number   Letter

### Personal Work and Study Habits Evaluation

_____   _____   Use of time in class

_____   _____   Use of time outside of class

_____   _____   Individual contribution to the group project research

_____   _____   Contribution to my group's final presentation

_____   _____   Team work: ability to lead or be led, as my group assignment dictated

_____   _____   Attention to accuracy and completeness

_____   _____   Attention to neatness

### Knowledge Gained and Ability Demonstrated

_____   _____   Knowledge of E. coli (cause, symptoms, treatment, prognosis)

_____   _____   Knowledge of HUS (cause, symptoms, treatment, prognosis)

_____   _____   Knowledge of infectious disease transmission

_____   _____   Knowledge of community interaction in a time of crisis

_____   _____   Ability to evaluate data to find significant information

_____   _____   Ability to see relationships among pieces of information

_____   _____   Ability to find an appropriate course of action

### Team Leaders Only

_____ _____ My ability to organize and assign workloads

_____ _____ My ability to accept suggestions from other team members

_____ _____ My ability to keep our team working in a cooperative, friendly manner

_____ _____ My ability to keep our team working on task

_____ _____ Overall quality or level of excellence of my leadership skills

### Other Team Members Only

_____ _____ My ability to accept my assigned workload

_____ _____ My ability to see what needs to be done and offer constructive suggestions

_____ _____ My ability to complete my assigned work load on time

_____ _____ My ability to work as a cooperative and friendly team member

_____ _____ My overall ability to follow

### ✎ My comments about this unit:

_____

_____

_____

_____

_____

_____

_____

_____

_____

_____

# Fuzzy Challenge Procedures

A fuzzy challenge is called fuzzy because what you need to do to succeed in the assignment is not clear at the start of the exercise. To begin everything seems a little bit fuzzy and undefined.

Fuzzy challenge assignments are very much like real life situations. Many times owners, directors, and employees in businesses and organizations are presented with a task (a challenge) that needs to be completed, but they don't have the necessary information or a specific plan to successfully complete the assignment. The goal of their assignment may be to "increase sales" or "find a cure" or "make the client happy" or "design a new program to meet a specific need." However, they may not know exactly what steps must be taken to accomplish the goal.

Before the assignment can be completed, the people working on it must discover what they need to know to be successful. They must design a plan to accomplish the task. Finally, they must implement their plan. There may be several different but acceptable ways of accomplishing the goal.

It is also quite possible that there are other individuals or teams working on the same project without their knowledge. Coming up with a solution to the assignment that is better than other individuals or groups, may mean a raise, a promotion or even the success or failure of the company or organization.

Here are some basic steps used to successfully complete a fuzzy challenge:

**1. Define** → Restate the assignment in specific terms.
List areas where you need more knowledge.

**2. Design** → Determine what needs to be done.
Determine how it will be done.
Determine who will do each thing.

**3. Do** → Do it.

**4. Determine potential for success** → Repeat steps 1 – 3 for areas that are still not exactly as you want them to be

**5. Debrief** → Analyze the success of your project.

# Mystery Disease

The Barrow County Fair ended on Monday,
September 3, and school started for the students of
rural Jamestown on the following Wednesday.
Some of the newer people in the community
didn't quite understand why school didn't start
until after the fair had closed. They had not lived
in the community long enough to share
everyone's fascination with whose calves, lambs,
and hogs did best in the 4H competition at the fair.

However, for most people in Jamestown, the
county fair was the high point of the year. It was a
chance to renew acquaintances, engage
in some friendly rivalry, and of course, eat fair food. Over half of the students in the
county showed animals at the fair and everybody (except for some of the newer kids and
those who are at church camp that week) went to the fair.

There is no way school could start until two days after the fair. It took that long to
get animals back home, put away projects, and clean up everything, not to mention a
day for everyone to try to catch their breath and get ready for the first day of school.

There was only one elementary school in Jamestown. There were two classes for
each grade, from kindergarten through sixth grade – a total of about 275 students.
School spirit was high at Jamestown. In each grade there was a trophy awarded to the
room that had the best grades for the grading period. There was even a stuffed lion, the
school mascot, that traveled to the room that had the best attendance each week. Not
only did they get the lion in their room, but everyone in the winning room got free ice
cream one day the following week.

That's why Mrs. Carl, the principal, thought it seemed rather strange when parents
started calling in the first morning of school to report that their children were ill. Most
indicated that their child or children either had a "touch of the flu" or had come down
with "some kind of a stomach bug." Only one mother mentioned that her daughter had a
fever; however, all parents mentioned severe stomach cramps and diarrhea. Some
mentioned vomiting.

Susie Thompson's mother thought Susie
"picked up a bug at church camp and gave it to
her brother Charlie." Neither of them would be
in school on the first day, and Charlie was
really upset. He had perfect attendance in both
fourth and fifth grade. He was especially
looking forward to school starting, since he had
been grounded last week and wasn't allowed to
go to the fair.

When Mrs. Carl finally finished talking with parents, she realized that seven students were going to be absent with the flu or something else, on the first day of school. That seemed like too much of a coincidence, so she called her friend Donna Burke, an emergency room nurse, to ask if she should be alarmed or if she was just overreacting.

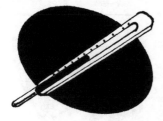

Mrs. Burke seemed seriously concerned when she heard about seven children with similar symptoms. She became even more concerned when she went to work that day at the Barrow County Hospital and found out that an elderly lady and two small children from a nearby town had been treated earlier in the day for similar symptoms.

The elderly lady and one of the children had been given Imodium AD to stop the diarrhea and had been sent home. The other child, however, was still in the emergency room. Her stomach cramps were severe and her diarrhea was bloody. The nursing staff was beginning to think it should have treated the first two patients differently and was wondering if they were about to see some kind of an epidemic.

By the end of the day, four of the seven students who missed the first day of school at Jamestown Elementary had been brought to the emergency room by their parents. The nurses knew there was trouble in Barrow County.

# The Challenge

Your challenge comes in two parts. Your response to part one should take no more than one class period.

➤ **Part One**
- Your group will act as the nursing staff of Barrow County Hospital.
- Using the Internet or other resources at your disposal, develop a tentative diagnosis of what may be wrong with these sick people.
- Present your findings to Dr. Billman (your teacher), the county health commissioner.

➤ **Part Two**
- Once your staff and Dr. Billman have come to an agreement on a tentative diagnosis, your role will change for part two.
- Your group will become county health inspectors at the Barrow County Health Department. You report directly to Dr. Billman.
- At that point you will receive your instructions for the second part of your assignment from Dr. Billman.

# MEMO

Date:      Thursday, September 6
From:      Doctor Billman
To:        All Barrow County health inspectors
Re:        Recent apparent E. coli outbreak

I was contacted last night by the nursing staff at Barrow County Hospital. Within a 16-hour period yesterday, six young children between the ages of 4 and 11 and one 68-year-old female, who all presented symptoms consistent with the onset of Escherichia Coli 0157:H7, were seen in the emergency room. Stool samples have been sent to a lab in Chicago, but results may not be back for awhile. Until we hear differently from the lab, we will proceed under the assumption that this is indeed an E. coli outbreak.

Four of the children seen at the emergency room are from Jamestown. The other two children and the older woman are from Bellburg, in Box County. None of the children the nurses saw attended school yesterday. The nurses have an unconfirmed report that several other children were absent from school in Jamestown yesterday.

If this apparent outbreak becomes as serious as it appears, we could easily end up with one or two dozen cases in a very short time. I don't need to tell you what the complications from that could be!

Please take immediate steps to interview all victims and their families as soon as possible. While you are completing your interviews, begin making your assessment of the situation and plans for your response.

By one week from today (September 13) you must do the following:

**1**. Determine the most probable source (or sources) of the E. coli outbreak. Be able to explain your theory and defend your ideas with hard evidence, research of appropriate literature, and logical reasoning.

**2**. Develop a plan to reduce or eliminate the possibility of a similar outbreak in the future. This plan must address all possible sources of the disease that you think may be responsible for the recent outbreak. Your plan must also take into consideration the values and needs of all persons involved.

You will report your findings on items one and two to me on September 13. Please be prepared for everyone on your staff to make an oral presentation. Your presentation should be supported with a written report, along with charts, maps, interview results, and any other materials you think appropriate.

In addition to these two tasks, you will do the following third task.

**3**. Develop a program for students in a lower grade designed to make them aware of:
  ▸ the dangers of E. coli and similar diseases
  ▸ ways they can be infected
  ▸ things they can do to keep themselves from getting sick from E. coli or similar diseases
  Do this without scaring your audience.

I will tell each team which grade levels to prepare for. You should be prepared to let me see this program on September 13. At a later date, you will make your presentation to your assigned class. Consider using visual aids or technology in your program to add interest. You want your audience to remember what you've said.

I remain available to talk with team leaders as necessary.

Dr. Billman

**Note:**
The information you need will be provided on contagious disease reports. You do not have to actually interview anybody. Each report may be considered the written results of an interview that was conducted by a member of your team.

# LINCOLN COUNTY

# Gazette

*Serving your county since 1931*

**SPECIAL ISSUE**

*"Contact health
care officials :
8:00-8:00 p.m.
123-456-7890"*

# E. Coli May Be Culprit at Fair

*By Susan Sanchez*
*NP News Service, PA*

**O**ver 320 people have reported becoming ill after attending the Lincoln County fair. State health officials have not ruled out the possibility that many of those suffering flu-like symptoms may have contracted E. coli, a potentially deadly bacterial infection.

**F**ourteen children and two adults have been admitted to General Hospital for observation and treatment after their symptoms worsened. Of those admitted, three have already been confirmed as E. coli. Officials are waiting for results on the others.

**M**eanwhile, county and state health officials are testing food and water samples that were collected from throughout the fairgrounds before the fair closed yesterday. While fair officials insisted that they have followed state guidelines

for food and water safety at the fair, suspicion surrounds two or three food vendors whose food service trailers have previously been cited for health violations.

**S**everal strains of E. coli bacteria normally live in the intestines of humans and warm-blooded animals. Most are harmless and some even aid in digestion. However , including 0157:H7, can cause sickness and in some cases can have deadly complications.

# SCOTTSVILLE TIMES

## E. Coli Outbreak Linked to Shawnee County Fair In Scottsville

*Duane Whiterspoon*
*Capitol Bureau*
*Oklahoma City, OK*

Doctors at several Oklahoma City area hospitals are coordinating their investigations of an apparent outbreak of E. coli linked to the Shawnee County Fair. Currently, two of the cases have been confirmed and four other patients are still being tested.

Three-year-old Mary Paxton appears to be one of the most seriously affected. She attended the fair twice and became ill several days after her last visit. Mary's mother reported that her child suffered from abdominal pain and bloody diarrhea.

Dr. Marianne Kindstein of the Oklahoma Children's Critical Care Clinic said that it could take from two to seven days after exposure to the E. coli bacteria for symptoms to begin. She stressed that "patients should get medical attention as soon as possible after the onset of symptoms, because E. coli can lead to kidney failure, which is the most serious complication from the bacterial infection."

Doctors have seen patients from several towns and cities throughout Shawnee County and expect to see more in the near future.

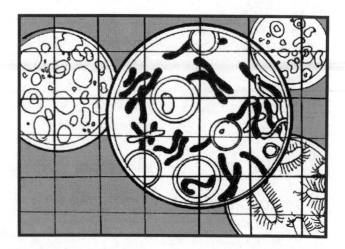

*E.coli virus under magnification*

# *Barrow County*
## Contagious Disease Report - Form CF

| To be used when investigating outbreaks that may be related to the County Fairgrounds |
| --- |

Case number   2001CF09AMB1785

Note:  The person represented on this form is ill.

Name of person represented on this form:   Susie Thompson

Other person(s) answering questions on this form:   Mrs. Thompson, Susie's mother

Check all statements that apply.

- ☐ Attended the fair   She was at the Baptist church camp through Friday evening.
- ☐ Played games
    - ☐ duck pond game
    - ☐ basketball game
    - ☐ ping pong ball/goldfish game
    - ☐ ring the bell game

- ☐ Ate fair food
    - ☐ homemade ice cream
    - ☐ elephant ears
    - ☐ hamburger

Contact with animals at the fair
   - ☐ cattle barn
   - ☐ goat barn
   - ☐ petting zoo
   - ☐ pony ride

Initial symptoms
   - ☑ diarrhea
   - ☑ stomach cramps
   - ☐ vomiting
   - ☐ fever

Contagious Disease Report  page 2

Case number ___2001CF09AMB1785___

Name of person represented on this form: ___Susie Thompson___

Other information obtained from the interview:

Susie Thompson attended church camp with her friend Donna Jones. She first complained of diarrhea and stomach cramps on Sunday morning. Her mother describes her as a really sweet girl, who adores her big brother. Even though her big brother (Charlie) seems to get into trouble a lot, he really looks after Susie. He shares everything with her and won't let others tease or bother her. When Susie came home from camp on Friday evening she brought Charlie a bag of candy. He shared the candy with her. They divided them up and when there was one extra red one, Charlie pretended to eat it but then gave it to Susie.

<u>Health inspector's personal note:</u>
This seems like a very nice family.

Mrs. Thompson seems to think Susie picked up a "stomach bug" at church camp. She remembers Charlie having the same thing a couple of years ago, when he came home from camp.

<u>Health inspector's question:</u>
Did anybody from the family go to the fair this year?

<u>Mrs. Thompson:</u>
Yes, the children's father judged the goat show.

<u>Health inspector's question:</u>
Did he bring home any fair food?

<u>Mrs. Thompson:</u>
No.

# *Barrow County*
## Contagious Disease Report - Form CF

To be used when investigating outbreaks that may be related to the County Fairgrounds

Case number ___2001CF09AMB2597___

Note: The person represented on this form is ill.

Name of person represented on this form: ___Charlie Thompson___

Other person(s) answering questions on this form: ___Mrs. Thompson, Charlie's mother___

Check all statements that apply.

- ☐ Attended the fair ___was grounded___
- ☐ Played games
    - ☐ duck pond game
    - ☐ basketball game
    - ☐ ping pong ball/goldfish game
    - ☐ ring the bell game

- ☐ Ate fair food
    - ☐ homemade ice cream
    - ☐ elephant ears
    - ☐ hamburger

- ☐ Contact with animals at the fair
    - ☐ cattle barn
    - ☐ goat barn
    - ☐ petting zoo
    - ☐ pony ride

Initial symptoms
- ☑ diarrhea
- ☑ stomach cramps
- ☐ vomiting
- ☐ fever

Contagious Disease Report

Case number    2001CF09AMB2597

Name of person represented on this form:    Charlie Thompson

Other information obtained from the interview:

Charlie seems to be a very active sixth grader.

Health inspector's personal note:
As I arrived, the first words from Mrs. Thompson were, "He's not in trouble again is he?" Mrs. Thompson indicated that Charlie is really a very bright boy, he just doesn't always think before acting. He really likes school and was upset than she wouldn't let him go to school sick. Mrs. Thompson seems to think he caught the "stomach bug" from his sister, who just got back from camp.

Health inspector's question:
Did Charlie go to the fair?

Mrs. Thompson:
"No, he was grounded and couldn't leave the farm. He spent most of the week taking care of the goats and going fishing. He may be grounded till Halloween. He says he fell out of the rowboat, but I think he just went swimming without a buddy. For being so smart in school he sure doesn't think when it counts! But then he turns around and does something sweet for his sister. He came home soaking wet from the pond, just as his sister came home from camp. He chased her around the yard, but never really tried to catch her. He wouldn't even take the bag of candy she brought him. He insisted that they share it. They took turns choosing colors. When there was just one red one left, he pretended to eat it, but then handed it to her and took another color."

Health inspector's personal note:
Mrs. Thompson seemed to want to talk about her children all day, but I finally got the conversation back to the subject of the fair.

Health inspector's Question:
Did you attend the fair?

Mrs. Thompson:
"No, I don't like all the rides and noise."

**40**

# *Barrow County*
## Contagious Disease Report - Form CF

| To be used when investigating outbreaks that may be related to the County Fairgrounds |
| --- |

Case number __2001CF09AMB3348__

Note: The person represented on this form is ill.

Name of person represented on this form: __David Jones__

Other person(s) answering questions on this form: __Mrs. Jones, David's mother__

Check all statements that apply.

- ☑ Attended the fair
- ☑ Played games
    - ☐ duck pond game
    - ☐ basketball game
    - ☑ ping pong ball/goldfish game
    - ☐ ring the bell game

- ☑ Ate fair food
    - ☑ homemade ice cream
    - ☑ elephant ears
    - ☐ hamburger

- ☑ Contact with animals at the fair
    - ☑ cattle barn
    - ☐ goat barn
    - ☐ petting zoo
    - ☐ pony ride

Initial symptoms
- ☑ diarrhea
- ☑ stomach cramps
- ☐ vomiting
- ☐ fever

Contagious Disease Report

Case number   <u>2001CF09AMB3348</u>

Name of person represented on this form:   <u>David Jones</u>

Other information obtained from the interview:

David's mother thinks he caught something from his sister, Donna Jones, who was at camp with her friend, Susie Thompson. She said, "It seems like the kids always get something at camp."

<u>Health inspector's question</u>:
Did either of your children attend the fair?

<u>Mrs. Jones</u>:
"Yes, David and his friend Allen Johnson rode their bikes to the fair every day. It doesn't seem like David or Allen, either one, has many friends. David is pretty focused on his church activities, and, well, you know, Allen is a bit strange what with that obsessive compulsive stuff. Anyway, David parked his bike in the Johnsons' tack stall and usually helped Allen do some morning chores with his calves. Then he'd head straight over to get to the church's game booth before it opened. He helped there most of the day. He liked passing out ping pong balls and giving other kids their goldfish when they threw a ball that lands in a fish bowl."

<u>Health inspector's question</u>:
Do you know what foods David ate while he was at the fair?

<u>Mrs. Jones</u>:
He took Snackables with him and bought bottled water to drink. He doesn't really like fair food. In fact, I think the only food he bought was a milkshake instead of water one day. He also bought an elephant ear on the last day of the fair. Even then, he only tore off and ate two or three bites of it and brought the rest of it home for his sister who was just getting home from camp. She ate it, but I'm not sure how much she enjoyed it. She was pretty quiet, and I wonder now if maybe she was already coming down with something from camp.

# *Barrow County*
## Contagious Disease Report - Form CF

| To be used when investigating outbreaks that may be related to the County Fairgrounds |
| --- |

Case number __2001CF09AMB4128__

Note: The person represented on this form is ill.

Name of person represented on this form: __Donna Jones__

Other person(s) answering questions on this form: __Mrs. Jones, Donna's mother__

Check all statements that apply.

- ☐ Attended the fair  __She was at the Baptist church camp through Friday evening.__
- ☐ Played games
    - ☐ duck pond game
    - ☐ basketball game
    - ☐ ping pong ball/goldfish game
    - ☐ ring the bell game
- ☑ Ate fair food
    - ☐ homemade ice cream
    - ☑ elephant ears  __brought home by her brother__
    - ☐ hamburger
- ☐ Contact with animals at the fair
    - ☐ cattle barn
    - ☐ goat barn
    - ☐ petting zoo
    - ☐ pony ride

Initial symptoms
- ☑ diarrhea
- ☑ stomach cramps
- ☑ vomiting
- ☐ fever

Contagious Disease Report

Case number   2001CF09AMB4128

Name of person represented on this form:   Donna Jones


Other information obtained from the interview:

  See notes for her brother, David Jones.

# *Barrow County*
## Contagious Disease Report - Form CF

| To be used when investigating outbreaks that may be related to the County Fairgrounds |
| --- |

Case number ___2001CF09AMB5691___

___Note: The person represented on this form is **not** ill.___

Name of person represented on this form: ___Allen Johnson___

Other person(s) answering questions on this form: ___Mrs. Johnson, Allen's mother___

Check all statements that apply.

- ☑ Attended the fair
- ☑ Played games
    - ☑ duck pond game
    - ☑ basketball game
    - ☑ ping pong ball/goldfish game
    - ☑ ring the bell game
- ☑ Ate fair food
    - ☑ homemade ice cream
    - ☑ elephant ears
    - ☑ hamburger

- ☑ Contact with animals at the fair
    - ☑ cattle barn
    - ☑ goat barn
    - ☑ petting zoo
    - ☑ pony ride

Initial Symptoms

- ☐ diarrhea
- ☐ stomach cramps
- ☐ vomiting
- ☐ fever

Contagious Disease Report

Case number   2001CF09AMB5691

Name of person represented on this form:   Allen Johnson

Other information obtained from the interview:

Allen attended the fair every day to show and take care of his cattle and to help his father set up the Kiwanis club rubber duck pond. Mrs. Johnson said, "Other than when he was going back and forth to the fair, with his friend David Jones, he pretty much stayed to himself. He really appreciates David's friendship. David is one of the few people who accept the behaviors that result from Allen's Obsessive Compulsive Disorder. You know how cruel children can be. In fact, when Allen's steer won best of class in showmanship, some of the kids teased him and said the only thing in the county cleaner than Allen was his cow. That really hurt his feelings. Allen did a lot of stuff at the fair, but he pretty much did it by himself.

Health inspector's note:
Since Allen had spent so much time with his friend David Jones, who is ill, I thought I would interview Allen and his family, even though he seems to be perfectly healthy.

# *Barrow County*
## Contagious Disease Report - Form CF

| To be used when investigating outbreaks that may be related to the County Fairgrounds |
| --- |

Case number ___2001CF09AMB6523___

Note: The person represented on this form is ill.

Name of person represented on this form: ___LuAnne Brown___

Other person(s) answering questions on this form: ___Mr. Brown, LuAnne's father___

Check all statements that apply.

- ☑ Attended the fair
- ☐ Played games
    - ☐ duck pond game
    - ☐ basketball game
    - ☐ ping pong ball/goldfish game
    - ☐ ring the bell game

- ☑ Ate fair food
    - ☑ homemade ice cream
    - ☑ elephant ears
    - ☑ hamburger

- ☑ Contact with animals at the fair
    - ☐ cattle barn
    - ☐ goat barn
    - ☐ petting zoo
    - ☑ pony ride

Initial symptoms
- ☐ diarrhea
- ☑ stomach cramps
- ☑ vomiting
- ☐ fever

Contagious Disease Report

Case number   2001CF09AMB6523

Name of person represented on this form:   LuAnne Brown

Other Information obtained from the interview:

<u>Health inspector's personal note:</u>
I talked with LuAnne's father, Mr. Brown, but he seemed relatively unconcerned about his daughter's illness, and he was not very talkative.

LuAnne attended the fair with her family on the last day. According to her father, she had a great time. The pony rides were her favorite thing, along with homemade ice cream, cotton candy, French fries and the caramel corn. She got sick right after going to the fair.

Her father indicated that she had a "stomach ache." She vomited a couple of times that evening but seemed better the next day. He thinks her mother was being a bit overprotective when she kept LuAnne home the first day of school.

# MEMO

Date:      Friday, September 7
From:      Doctor Billman
To:        All Barrow County health inspectors
Re:        Recent apparent E. coli outbreak

This outbreak seems to be getting more serious. Please take the following actions:

**1**. Make every effort to interview as many victims and their families as possible. You may even want to interview some people who are not ill, but who have similar histories over the last week or so.

**2**. You should probably plan to work late this evening and cancel any plans you have for this Saturday. This looks serious.

**3**. I've obtained a map of the fairgrounds as it was set up this year. You may want to review the fair layout and make suggestions for next year.

Team Leaders

   Be certain to schedule some time today to make sure your staff is updated on the most current information regarding the spread of E. coli.

   Be especially certain they are aware of potential complications from the disease and are ready to suggest immediate action to parents and health care professionals if any complications appear. You may make appropriate emergency action suggestions without taking the time to consult with me.

   I remain available to talk with team leaders as necessary.

*Dr. Billman*

*handout 3.2*

# THE CITY SENTINEL

**VOLUME 9, number 7**
Ottawa City
Circulation editor
(123) 456-7890

PREVENTION
For You and Your
Family

# Family Sues Over E. Coli at Fun Fair

*David White Eagle*
*Ottawa City, ID —*

Robert and Linda Connors have filed a lawsuit in Big Falls County Court alleging that they and three of their four children became seriously ill as a result of attending the county fair last

and Ella's Beefy Burgers food trailer. Several other people who ate hamburgers from Sam and Ella's also became ill after the fair. Hamburger from the same food trailer tested positive for the E. coli bacteria at another county fair just three weeks before the Big Falls Fair.

The family contends that county officials knew, or should have known, about the danger posed by this food vendor and should be held responsible for neglecting to protect the public's health. The family's attorney has not ruled out suing the state health department as well.

August. The defendants named in the suit include the county commissioners, the fair board, the county health department and an out-of-town food vendor.

The Connors family is seeking twenty-three million dollars in damages. They claim they became ill after eating E. coli tainted food from the Sam

Mr. and Mrs. Connors and two of their ill children have apparently recovered from their bout with E. coli. However, their youngest son Jeremy remains in guarded condition at Children's Hospital, where he has developed kidney disease as a result of the E. coli infection.

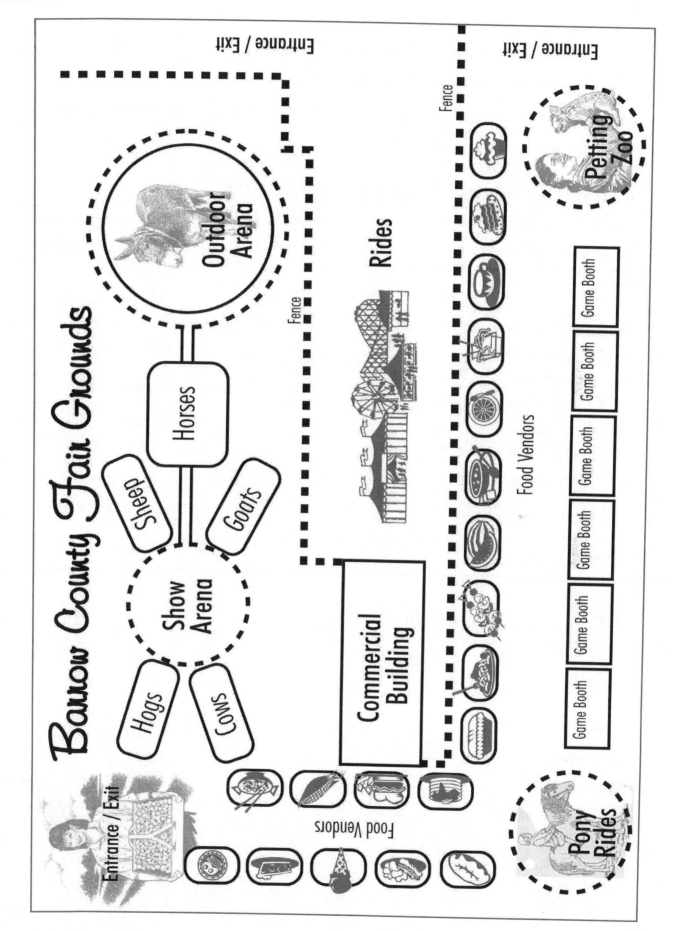

Barrow County Fair Grounds

Entrance / Exit

Entrance / Exit

Entrance / Exit

Fence

Fence

Outdoor Arena

Horses

Sheep

Goats

Show Arena

Hogs

Cows

Rides

Commercial Building

Food Vendors

Game Booth
Game Booth
Game Booth
Game Booth
Game Booth
Game Booth
Game Booth
Game Booth

Petting Zoo

Pony Rides

Food Vendors

Entrance / Exit

# 𝓑𝒶𝓇𝓇𝑜𝓌 𝒞𝑜𝓊𝓃𝓉𝓎

## Contagious Disease Report - Form CF

| To be used when investigating outbreaks that may be related to the County Fairgrounds |
|---|

Case number __2001CF09AMB7227__

    Note: The person represented on this form is ill.

Name of person represented on this form: __Jonathan Miller__

Other person(s) answering questions on this form: __Mrs. Miller, Jonathan's mother__

Check all statements that apply.

- ☑ Attended the fair
- ☑ Played games
    - ☐ duck pond game
    - ☑ basketball game
    - ☑ ping pong ball/goldfish game
    - ☑ ring the bell game

- ☑ Ate fair food
    - ☐ homemade ice cream
    - ☑ elephant ears
    - ☑ hamburger

- ☑ Contact with animals at the fair
    - ☑ cattle barn
    - ☐ goat barn
    - ☐ petting zoo
    - ☐ pony ride

Initial symptoms
- ☑ diarrhea
- ☑ stomach cramps
- ☐ vomiting
- ☐ fever

Contagious Disease Report

Case number __2001CF09AMB7227__

Name of person represented on this form: __Jonathan Miller__

Other information obtained from the interview:

According to Jonathan's mother, Mrs. Miller, Jonathan lives for the fair.

<u>Health inspector's personal note:</u>
When I asked Jonathan and his mother what he did at the fair, they listed almost all the activities.

The Millers moved here just a couple of years ago. They said they did not have a fair near the city where they previously lived, so they had never been to the fair before. Jonathan says he wants to be a farmer or an astronaut when he grows up. Jonathan will do everything there is to do at the fair, except for things he considers "just for little kids."

He was at the fair on both the opening and closing days as well as one afternoon during the week.

# *Barrow County*
## Contagious Disease Report - Form CF

> To be used when investigating outbreaks that may be related to the County Fairgrounds

Case number ___2001CF09AMB8299___

   Note: The person represented on this form is ill.

Name of person represented on this form: ___Mary Smith___

Other person(s) answering questions on this form: ___Mrs. Smith, Mary's mother___

___and her grandmother, Mrs. McCoy___

Check all statements that apply.

- ☑ Attended the fair
- ☐ Played games
    - ☐ duck pond game
    - ☐ basketball game
    - ☐ ping pong ball/goldfish game
    - ☐ ring the bell game

- ☑ Ate fair food
    - ☑ homemade ice cream
    - ☐ elephant ears
    - ☑ hamburger

- ☑ Contact with animals at the fair
    - ☐ cattle barn
    - ☐ goat barn
    - ☐ petting zoo
    - ☑ pony ride

Initial symptoms
- ☑ diarrhea
- ☑ stomach cramps
- ☐ vomiting
- ☐ fever

Contagious Disease Report

Case number  2001CF09AMB8299

Name of person represented on this form:  Mary Smith

Other information obtained from the interview:

<u>Health inspector's personal note:</u>

I interviewed Mary, her mother and her grandmother in the Smith home. Mr. McCoy was napping and I wasn't able to talk with him. However, I was able to determine that he did not go to the fair. He had worked too hard in his garden and needed to rest that day.

Mary Smith has a Bellburg address and phone number. Bellburg is just across the county line in Box County; however, the Jamestown School District crosses the county line in a couple of places and the Smith family farm is in the Jamestown School District. The Smith farm is really the old McCoy place. Mary's mother is a McCoy, and her grandparents still live in the older house on the farm. Everybody in the family, including Mary's grandparents, went to the Jamestown School, so they always go to the Barrow County Fair instead of the one in Box County.

Mary attended the fair with her Grammy McCoy on senior citizens day, which was on Sunday, September 2. Her grandmother's leg was bothering her and the fair food was too greasy for her, so they didn't stay very long. Mary rode the ponies and the merry-go-round. Her grandmother bought her a hamburger and a milk shake, and then they left. They stopped at The Garden Spot, a new restaurant, where Mary got a Pepsi and Mrs. McCoy had the soup and sandwich special (she had them hold the lettuce and tomato). Mrs. McCoy laughed about how Mary certainly didn't get her love of vegetables from her grandmother. Mary loves vegetables, especially tomatoes right off the vine, which she and her Grampy McCoy raise together. Mrs. McCoy insisted on telling me all about the new restaurant and recommended it highly.

# *Barrow County*
## Contagious Disease Report - Form CF

| To be used when investigating outbreaks that may be related to the County Fairgrounds |
| --- |

Case number __2001CF09AMB9435__

___Note: The person represented on this form is ill.___

Name of person represented on this form: __Anthony Green__

Other person(s) answering questions on this form: __Mr. Green, Anthony's father__

Check all statements that apply.

- ☑ Attended the fair
- ☑ Played games
    - ☑ duck pond game
    - ☐ basketball game
    - ☐ ping pong ball/goldfish game
    - ☐ ring the bell game

- ☑ Ate fair food
    - ☑ homemade ice cream
    - ☑ elephant ears
    - ☐ hamburger

- ☑ Contact with animals at the fair
    - ☐ cattle barn
    - ☐ goat barn
    - ☐ petting zoo
    - ☑ pony ride

Initial symptoms
- ☑ diarrhea
- ☑ stomach cramps
- ☐ vomiting
- ☐ fever

**56**

Contagious Disease Report

Case number __2001CF09AMB9435__

Name of person represented on this form: __Anthony Green__


Other information obtained from the interview:

Anthony Green is a very bright young boy. His parents homeschooled him for kindergarten, and he will be the youngest boy in his first grade class at Jamestown Elementary School. His father said that the two of them attended the fair with Anthony's mother.

The family rode rides together and had some fair food. Anthony won a teddy bear in the duck pond game, but other than that, Mr. Green couldn't think of anything out of the ordinary. Anthony became ill after attending the fair. His mother took him to their family doctor, but he said it was probably just a combination of fair food and excitement about first day of school at the public school.

Health inspector's note:
Mrs. Green was working when I conducted the interview.

# Barrow County

### Contagious Disease Report - Form CF

| To be used when investigating outbreaks that may be related to the County Fairgrounds |
| --- |

Case number   2001CF09AB10881

Note: The person represented on this form is **not** ill.

Name of person represented on this form:   Mrs. McCoy

Other person(s) answering questions on this form:   none

Check all statements that apply.

- ☑ Attended the fair
- ☐ Played games
    - ☐ duck pond game
    - ☐ basketball game
    - ☐ ping pong ball/goldfish game
    - ☐ ring the bell game

- ☑ Ate fair food
    - ☐ homemade ice cream
    - ☐ elephant ears
    - ☑ hamburger sandwich

- ☐ Contact with animals at the fair
    - ☐ cattle barn
    - ☐ goat barn
    - ☐ petting zoo
    - ☐ pony ride

Initial symptoms
- ☐ diarrhea
- ☐ stomach cramps
- ☐ vomiting
- ☐ fever

© **Prufrock Press Inc.**- Mystery Disease

Contagious Disease Report

Case number ___2001CF09AB10881___

Name of person represented on this form: ___Mrs. McCoy___


Other information obtained from the interview:

    See notes for her granddaughter, Mary Smith.

# MEMO

Date:     Saturday, September 8
From:     Doctor Billman
To:       All Barrow County health inspectors
Re:       Recent apparent E. coli outbreak

Good morning. Thank you for your commitment to solving this crisis. I know several of you had family activities planned for today, and I'm grateful for your willingness to work on a Saturday.

I've been receiving calls from concerned citizens, from the hospital, and from John Brandon over at the <u>Barrow County Sentinel</u>.

Some citizens are on the verge of panic. Donna Burke said Susie Thompson had been getting better but has taken a turn for the worse and was admitted to the hospital late last night with severe dehydration and a rash. John has gotten calls from several irate citizens and has already started getting "letters to the editor." He is planning on publishing the letters starting Monday and wants a statement from us.

Stacy Heilman, the fair board president, has gotten some nasty phone calls from vendors, as well as from local citizens. People are starting to blame other people in an effort to protect their own reputations. She wants quick action on our part.

It is just as important that you find out who is **not** responsible, as it is that you find the source of this outbreak. We do not want to accuse an innocent party of causing or spreading this pathogen. To implicate an innocent party could put this office at risk of a lawsuit.

In short, I need you to redouble your efforts. Continue doing interviews and analyzing the situation. I'd like to see you complete your interviews by Monday and have some tentative conclusions by Tuesday.

I remain available to talk with team leaders as necessary.

*Dr. Billman*

# *Barrow County*
## Contagious Disease Report - Form CF

| To be used when investigating outbreaks that may be related to the County Fairgrounds |
|---|

Case number ___2001CF09AB11235___

_____Note: The person represented on this form is ill._____

Name of person represented on this form: __Bruce Donaldson_____

Other person(s) answering questions on this form: __Mrs. Donaldson, Bruce's mother__


Check all statements that apply.

- ☑ Attended the fair
- ☑ Played games
  - ☐ duck pond game
  - ☑ basketball game
  - ☐ ping pong ball/goldfish game
  - ☑ ring the bell game

- ☑ Ate fair food
  - ☑ homemade ice cream
  - ☐ elephant ears
  - ☑ hamburger sandwich

- ☑ Contact with animals at the fair
  - ☐ cattle barn
  - ☐ goat barn
  - ☐ petting zoo
  - ☑ pony ride

Initial symptoms
- ☑ diarrhea
- ☑ stomach cramps
- ☑ vomiting
- ☐ fever

Case number ___2001CF09AB11235___

Name of person represented on this form: ___Bruce Donaldson___

Other information obtained from your interview:

Mrs. Donaldson took Bruce to ride the ponies on the last day of the fair. Bruce was worried that he wouldn't get to ride them this year because he is getting almost too big for them. She noted, though, that he's not quite big enough to ring the bell with that big hammer thing. She doesn't think his sickness is related to the fair. She seems proud of the fact that Bruce is a very responsible boy. She said, "He behaved himself at the fair, didn't eat too much junk food, and always washed his hands before he did eat something."

She's also proud of the way he is willing to help his Grandpa Smith milk the cows. She said he rode his bike over to his grandpa's dairy farm and helped with the afternoon milking at least two or three times a week this summer. She explained, "He gets to help wash the equipment. His grandpa calls him Mr. Clean, because he does such a good job. I think the high point of the summer was when his grandpa showed Bruce how he had learned to milk by hand when he was a boy. Dad said Bruce took right to it. Anyway, after they were done with the milking lesson, Bruce helped his grandpa fix some equipment."

Health inspector's note:
I got the impression Mrs. Donaldson was going to go on and on about interesting things that weren't related to the current outbreak, so I politely excused myself and told her I had to interview other folks.

# *Barrow County*

## Contagious Disease Report - Form CF

| To be used when investigating outbreaks that may be related to the County Fairgrounds |
|---|

Case number __2001CF09AB12219__

_____Note: The person represented on this form is ill._____

Name of person represented on this form: __Mr. Black_____

Other person(s) answering questions on this form: __none_____

Check all statements that apply.

- ☑ Attended the fair
- ☑ Played games
  - ☐ duck pond game
  - ☐ basketball game   __Mr. Black did not play, but mentioned watching his__
    __daughter play for quite a while.__
  - ☐ ping pong ball/goldfish game
  - ☑ ring the bell game
- ☐ Ate fair food
  - ☐ homemade ice cream
  - ☐ elephant ears
  - ☐ hamburger
- ☐ Contact with animals at the fair
  - ☐ cattle barn
  - ☐ goat barn
  - ☐ petting zoo
  - ☐ pony ride

Initial symptoms

- ☑ diarrhea
- ☑ stomach cramps
- ☐ vomiting
- ☑ fever

Contagious Disease Report

Case number ___2001CF09AB12219___

Name of person represented on this form: ___Mr. Black___

Other information obtained from your interview:

Mr. Black was visibly upset when I interviewed him. He recently moved to Barrow County from Capitol City where he works as a vice president at Chronotech Industries. He is considering taking legal action against the county and the fair board because both he and his daughter became ill after attending the fair. He is also threatening to move out of "this 19th century hick town" and back to Capitol City. He stated, "You try to give your children a nice quiet safe place to live, and this is what happens! Yes, we attended the fair but we certainly didn't eat anything there. And "no" we didn't touch any of those animals. The only reason we went in the first place was to try to be neighborly. Donna is entering her freshman year at your school and she wanted to meet the basketball coach because she will be playing on the team this year. She won the limit of three large dolls at the basketball throw at the fair and did it in only four tries even with those small hoops."

Since they were both ill, I wanted to make sure they hadn't eaten anything. Mr. Black's answer was, "No, I already said we wouldn't be caught dead eating that sort of food. We don't even eat out in this town except at The Garden Spot where we ate after attending the fair. It's not the best, but it's the only restaurant in this town where one can get anything that remotely resembles a decent sprout salad. Otherwise we zip on down to Capitol City if we want to dine out or entertain guests. You didn't have to eat anything at that disgusting fair to get sick. The smells alone were enough to make decent people ill. I don't know why you people don't just cancel that silly animal fair and replace it with something civilized like an art or music fair. Maybe then you'd have a better class of people moving into this county."

When Mr. Black began to accuse our office of being responsible for his illness, I felt it was time to end the interview.

# *Barrow County*
## Contagious Disease Report - Form CF

To be used when investigating outbreaks that may be related to the County Fairgrounds

Case number ___2001CF09AB13944___

___Note: The person represented on this form is ill.___

Name of person represented on this form: ___Donna Black___

Other person(s) answering questions on this form: ___Mr. Black, Donna's father___

Check all statements that apply.

- ☑ Attended the fair ___with her father, Mr. Black___
- ☑ Played games
    - ☐ duck pond game
    - ☑ basketball game
    - ☐ ping pong ball/goldfish game
    - ☐ ring the bell game

- ☐ Ate fair food
    - ☐ homemade ice cream
    - ☐ elephant ears
    - ☐ hamburger

- ☐ Contact with animals at the fair
    - ☐ cattle barn
    - ☐ goat barn
    - ☐ petting zoo
    - ☐ pony ride

Initial symptoms
- ☑ diarrhea
- ☑ stomach cramps
- ☐ vomiting
- ☐ fever

Contagious Disease report

Case number   2001CF09AB13944

Name of person represented on this form:   Donna Black

Other information obtained from the interview:

See Mr. Black's interview.

# MEMO

Date: Monday, September 10
From: Doctor Billman
To: All Barrow County health inspectors
Re: Recent apparent E. coli outbreak

As you may have already heard, Susie Thompson passed away last night at Barrow County Hospital. She had seemingly recovered from her initial illness but was admitted to the hospital late Friday evening with severe dehydration. Her condition worsened during the day on Saturday. Her kidneys began failing rapidly and most of her major body systems shut down before she died.

I know you have worked hard this weekend, but we must increase our efforts, making sure that our assessment is both thorough and accurate. We do not want an innocent person or vendor implicated in this tragedy. Even more importantly, we do not want any other children or adults to die as a result of this situation.

Please do the following:

- Find out everything you can about what caused the death of the Thompson girl.
- Determine if there were any warning signs.
- Recheck all people who have been ill to see if any are showing signs of similar complications. Contact me **immediately** by memo or e-mail if you think something specific needs to be done to help someone.

I have noted your request for maps of the county. Aerial maps of the county are 10 to 15 years old and are very outdated. I have contacted AeroMap in Capitol City and have requested an aerial survey of the county. They have assured me that their planes will be in the air today and they will work through the night to have maps for us tomorrow. I remain available to talk with team leaders as necessary

*Dr. Billman*

**Note:**
At this point, your team's responses will determine the information you will receive from Dr. Billman. Not all groups will receive the same information.

# *Barrow County*
## Contagious Disease Report - Form CF

| To be used when investigating outbreaks that may be related to the County Fairgrounds |

Case number   2001CF09AB14582

Note: The person represented on this form is ill.

Name of person represented on this form:   Mr. McCoy

Other person(s) answering questions on this form:   none

Check all statements that apply.

- ☐ Attended the fair
- ☐ Played games
    - ☐ duck pond game
    - ☐ basketball game
    - ☐ ping pong ball/goldfish game
    - ☐ ring the bell game

- ☑ Ate fair food
    - ☐ homemade ice cream
    - ☑ elephant ears   brought home by his wife
    - ☐ hamburger

- ☐ Contact with animals at the fair
    - ☐ cattle barn
    - ☐ goat barn
    - ☐ petting zoo
    - ☐ pony ride

Initial symptoms
- ☑ diarrhea
- ☑ stomach cramps
- ☐ vomiting
- ☐ fever

Contagious Disease Report

Case number   <u>2001CF09AB14582</u>

Name of person represented on this form:   <u>Mr. McCoy</u>

Other information obtained from the interview:

<u>Health inspector's note</u>:
This is my second visit to the McCoy place.

I had been told previously that Mr. McCoy was napping because he was tired from working in his garden. Apparently he also had a "touch of something" and thought it was just a stomach bug. His doctor called the Health Department after seeing Mr. McCoy late on Saturday. His symptoms made me think I should visit him.

Mr. McCoy is a retired farmer who seemed a bit sad that he didn't get to attend the fair this year. He stated that his bum hip kept him close to home this year. "About all I've got now is my garden." He invited me to see it.

I was quite surprised to see how beautiful Mr. McCoy's garden looked. Even with all the rain we've had recently, his tomatoes were beautiful and showed no signs of tomato rot. He plucked a ripe tomato and offered it to me. When I declined, he pulled a saltshaker from his trousers, put some on the tomato and enjoyed what he called "the freshest vegetable this side of Heaven."

Mr. McCoy said that he would have liked to have gone to the fair with his granddaughter, Mary Smith, especially since she is the one who has helped him so much in the tomato patch.

He also misses seeing his old friend Elsie Johnson and wishes that his own children had wanted to run the McCoy farm the way the Johnson kids are taking care of Elsie's old place. He and Elsie used to compete for the best steer every year. Now the closest they get to steers is when the two of them shovel a load of manure into his truck each spring for the garden.

I asked Mr. McCoy if he had eaten any fair food and he said that his wife had brought home an elephant ear for him.

# *Barrow County*
## Contagious Disease Report - Form CF

| To be used when investigating outbreaks that may be related to the County Fairgrounds |
| --- |

Case number  __2001CF09AB15568__

Note: The person represented on this form is ill.

Name of person represented on this form:  __Darryl Harper__

Other person(s) answering questions on this form:  __Mrs. Harper, Darryl's mother__

Check all statements that apply.

- ☑ Attended the fair
- ☑ Played games
    - ☑ duck pond game
    - ☑ basketball game
    - ☐ ping pong ball/goldfish game
    - ☐ ring the bell game

- ☑ Ate fair food
    - ☐ homemade ice cream
    - ☐ elephant ears
    - ☑ hamburger

- ☑ Contact with animals at the fair
    - ☑ cattle barn
    - ☐ goat barn
    - ☐ petting zoo
    - ☐ pony ride

Initial symptoms
- ☑ diarrhea
- ☑ stomach cramps
- ☐ vomiting
- ☐ fever

© Prufrock Press Inc.- Mystery Disease

Contagious Disease Report

Case number __2001CF09AB15568__

Name of person represented on this form: __Darryl Harper__

Other information obtained from the interview:

Darryl's mother seemed at a loss to remember anything unusual about their trip to the fair. She said, "He really wasn't sick for all that long, and he will probably go back to school on Tuesday or Wednesday if his rash clears up." Mrs. Harper thinks he ate too many fresh peaches and he may be having a case of hives.

# *Barrow County*
## Contagious Disease Report - Form CF

| To be used when investigating outbreaks that may be related to the County Fairgrounds |
|---|

Case number ___2001CF09AB16337___

___Note: The person represented on this form is ill.___

Name of person represented on this form: ___Jennifer Hallon___

Other person(s) answering questions on this form:___Mrs. Hallon, Jennifer's mother___

Check all statements that apply.

- ☑ Attended the fair
- ☑ Played games
    - ☑ duck pond game
    - ☐ basketball game
    - ☐ ping pong ball/goldfish game
    - ☐ ring the bell game

- ☑ Ate fair food
    - ☑ homemade ice cream
    - ☐ elephant ears
    - ☑ hamburger

- ☑ Contact with animals at the fair
    - ☐ cattle barn
    - ☐ goat barn
    - ☑ petting zoo
    - ☑ pony ride

Initial symptoms
- ☑ diarrhea
- ☑ stomach cramps
- ☐ vomiting
- ☐ fever

**72**

© **Prufrock Press Inc**.- Mystery Disease

Contagious Disease Report

Case number ___2001CF09AB16337___

Name of person represented on this form: ___Jennifer Hallon___

Other information obtained from the interview:

Jennifer had symptoms similar to most of the other ill students. Her mother has heard about the outbreak and is very concerned for her daughter. Jennifer wants to be a forest ranger and work in the Rocky Mountains. Jennifer enjoyed the deer in the petting zoo and the pony rides. She said she felt like a park ranger when she was riding the ponies and feeding the deer. Mrs. Hallon is concerned that this illness may have tragic consequences in her daughter's life and wants us to tell her what to do.

Even though her daughter is back in school today (Monday, September 10), Mrs. Hallon seems to be overwhelmed with the fear that her daughter is going to die. She is even thinking of going to the school and taking Jennifer home early.

# *Barrow County*
## Contagious Disease Report - Form CF

| To be used when investigating outbreaks that may be related to the County Fairgrounds |
| --- |

Case number  2001CF09AB17268

Note: The person represented on this form is ill.

Name of person represented on this form:  Eileen Bradley

Other person(s) answering questions on this form:  Mr. Bradley, Eileen's father

Check all statements that apply.

- ☑ Attended the fair
- ☑ Played games
    - ☐ duck pond game
    - ☐ basketball game
    - ☑ ping pong ball/goldfish game
    - ☐ ring the bell game

- ☑ Ate fair food
    - ☑ homemade ice cream
    - ☐ elephant ears
    - ☑ hamburger

- ☑ Contact with animals at the fair
    - ☐ cattle barn
    - ☐ goat barn
    - ☐ petting zoo
    - ☑ pony ride

Initial symptoms
- ☑ diarrhea
- ☑ stomach cramps
- ☐ vomiting
- ☐ fever

**74**

Contagious Disease Report

Case number ___2001CF09AB17268___

Name of person represented on this form: ___Eileen Bradley_____

Other information obtained from the interview:

Mr. Bradley was disturbed by the news today but did not seem to be panicked by it.

He and his daughter Eileen went to the fair together. They pretty much did everything together, and he can't recall anything specific that seemed out of the ordinary.

Eileen seems to be getting better and will probably go to school tomorrow. Mr. Bradley seems more concerned about the school work she has missed than any long-term consequences of her illness.

# URGENT FAX

Date:     Monday, September 10 — 2:05 PM
From:     Doctor Billman
To:       All Barrow County health inspectors
Re:       Recent apparent E. coli outbreak

    I just got off the phone with John Brandon at the <u>Sentinel</u>. He said he is not going to print all the public letters today, but he will to have to run the story of the Thompson girl's death in tomorrow's paper, along with an editorial and at least one or two of the public letters he's received.

    He wants to include a response from us and can get it in the paper if we get something to him by 9:30 tomorrow morning, Tuesday, September 11.

    I have another appointment I must attend this evening, so I will be unable to write anything for the paper. I am, therefore, asking you to write a letter for the newspaper.

    By 9:20 tomorrow morning have a 100-200 word "letter to the public" on my desk that outlines our office's response to this crisis so far. Do not say anything that you do not know for sure but reassure the public by letting them know what we are doing and that we are making progress.

    I remain available to talk with team leaders as necessary.

*Dr. Billman*

**Note:**
At this point, your team's responses will determine the information you will receive from Dr. Billman. Not all groups will receive the same information.

# URGENT FAX

Date:      Monday, September 10 — 4:55 PM
From:     Doctor Billman
To:        All Barrow county health inspectors
Re:        Recent apparent E. coli outbreak

This has been a trying day and I want to thank each of you personally for your efforts. You are all working extremely well under difficult circumstances.

There have been no new cases of E. coli since last Thursday, which is a good sign.

More than half of the students who were ill have returned to class, although some parents are keeping their children (even those who have been healthy all along) home as a precaution. The Greens are considering withdrawing Anthony altogether and going back to homeschooling. Apparently as soon as he went to school he picked up a rash from somewhere. One or two parents pulled their children out of school as soon as they heard the news about the Thompson girl, even though their children are not ill.

We must take immediate steps to ease the fears of our citizens and to help avoid a full-blown panic. I welcome any suggestions you may have.

I remain available to talk with team leaders as necessary.

Dr. Billman

**Note:**
At this point, your team's responses will determine the next information you will receive from Dr. Billman. Not all groups will receive the same information.

# MEMO

Date:  Tuesday, September 11
From:  Doctor Billman
To:    All Barrow County health inspectors
Re:    Recent apparent E. coli outbreak

Thank you for your letter to the <u>Barrow County Sentinel</u>.

I understand that the paper will run the story of the Thompson girl's death today but will hold off printing public letters and an editorial until tomorrow. Your letter will be published later this week.

I've heard through the grapevine that the Green family is withdrawing Anthony from public school and going back to home schooling. Anthony's rash apparently got worse yesterday. They took him to their family doctor and the doctor wants him to spend a day or two in the hospital for observation. It seems he's having some mood changes and has become quite argumentative. Their doctor isn't sure if this has anything to do with the rash or if Anthony is having psychological problems regarding the death of a classmate.

I look forward to seeing your action plan this Thursday. I have obtained the maps of the county. You will find them with today's memo.

I remain available to talk with team leaders as necessary.

*Dr. Billman*

# Enlarged Partial Section of Map of Barrow County

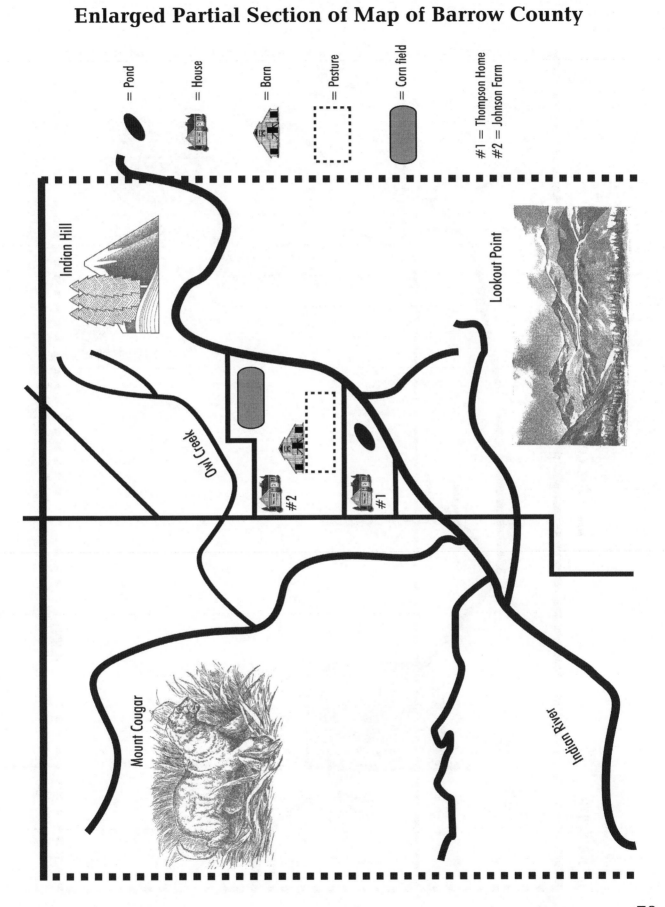

= Pond

= House

= Barn

= Pasture

= Corn field

#1 = Thompson Home
#2 = Johnson Farm

Indian Hill

Lookout Point

Owl Creek

#2

#1

Mount Cougar

Indian River

**79**

# Section of Barrow County

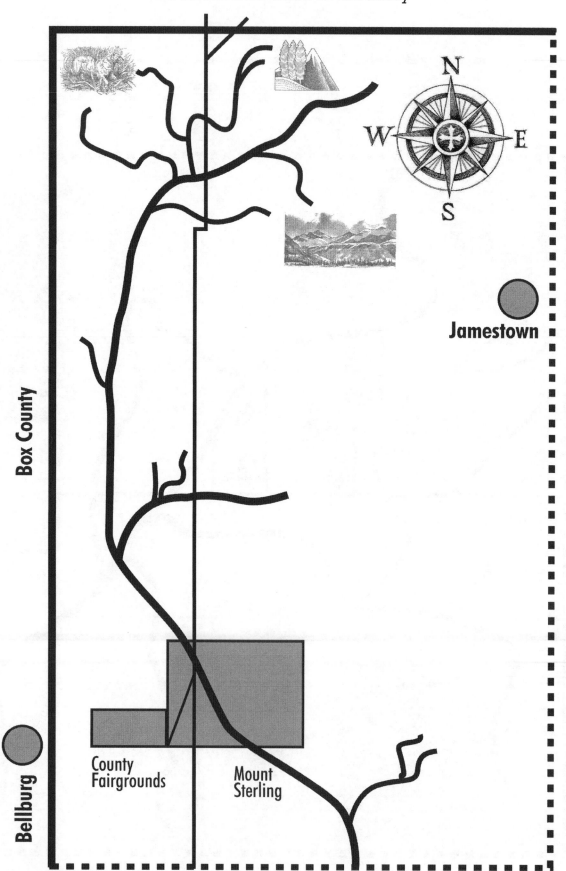

Box County

Bellburg

County
Fairgrounds

Mount
Sterling

Jamestown

# URGENT FAX

Date:    Tuesday, September 11 – 1:00 PM
From:    Doctor Billman
To:      All Barrow County health inspectors
Re:      Recent apparent E. coli outbreak

## For your immediate attention

I just got a call from Doctor Goldstein, Anthony Green's physician. Anthony has been transferred from a regular room at Barrow County Hospital to intensive care. He has begun dehydrating and there is some indication that his kidneys are beginning to fail.

Please give me your thoughts on the situation **immediately**. What are we missing here? Is there anybody else in immediate danger?

**We must get on top of this situation before it gets worse!**

*Dr. Billman*

**Note:**
At this point your team's responses will determine the next information you receive from Dr. Billman. Not all groups will receive the same information.

# MEMO

Date:     Wednesday, September 12
From:    Doctor Billman
To:       All Barrow County health inspectors
Re:       Recent apparent E. coli outbreak

## Critical Information

I'm saddened and upset to report I just got off the phone with Dr. Goldstein, who informed me that Anthony Green died early this morning. We all share the grief and agony experienced by the Green family.

I am <u>extremely</u> <u>concerned</u> that we were not able to help Dr. Goldstein make any lifesaving decisions. There may still be children at risk out there. Ask yourselves these questions:

✔ What are we missing?

✔ What are we doing to see that there are no more deaths?

**Please advise immediately regarding who you think may be at risk of developing similar complications.**

I will expect a response **<u>today</u>** and I will look forward to getting your complete report tomorrow.

I remain available to talk with team leaders as necessary.

*Dr. Billman*

# MEMO

Date:      Wednesday, September 12
From:      Doctor Billman
To:        All Barrow County health inspectors
Re:        Recent apparent E. coli outbreak

## Critical Information

Thank you for your rapid intervention on behalf of Anthony Green.

I'm happy to report that he has been transferred to the hospital in Capitol City as you suggested. He has been stabilized and is expected to make at least a partial, if not a full, recovery.

However, I am still <u>extremely</u> <u>concerned</u> that we did not catch his symptoms sooner. What are we doing to see that there are no more close calls? There may still be children at risk out there. Ask yourselves these questions:

✔ What are we missing?

✔ How can we prevent this outbreak from spreading?

**Please advise immediately regarding who you think may be at risk of developing similar complications.**

I will expect a response **<u>today</u>** and I will look forward to getting your complete report tomorrow.

I remain available to talk with team leaders as necessary.

*Dr. Billman*

# Barrow County Sentinel

Wednesday, September 12

## Editorial

As we consider the events of the past week, our community extends its sympathy to the family and friends of Susie Thompson. There can be no greater loss to our community than that of a child's life.

Community officials are currently using every means at their disposal to determine the cause or causes of the recent E. coli outbreak in Barrow County and are actively searching to find out if there is a link between this outbreak and the death of the Thompson girl. Until our health department officials have made a scientific determination of causes and any possible links, we urge the people of Barrow County to remain calm and not jump to conclusions. This is a time for thoughtful consideration, not for panic.

There have been rumors and accusations circulating throughout the county over the past several days. Most of these rumors have no basis in fact. While it

Is the policy of this paper to print letters expressing all viewpoints on an issue, our readers should remember that publishing a letter in the *Barrow County Sentinel* does not imply an endorsement by the newspaper of the ideas expressed in that letter.

We would remind our readers of the 127-year history of our county fair, its exemplary record of health and safety, and the outstanding dedication of our fair board members. We have the utmost confidence in their record of achievement and their sense of commitment to a safe and healthy fair experience for all who attend.

We must, however, face the fact that people have gotten ill at a time that corresponds with this year's fair. While we are not drawing any conclusions, we must consider all possibilities and support our health department as it investigates this tragic situation.

# Barrow County Sentinel
Wednesday, September 12

## Letters to the Editor

Dear Editor,

I would like to join our friends and neighbors in expressing our deepest sympathies to the family and friends of Susie Thompson. The members of the Dairy Council of Barrow County are all part of this community. We all work and live here, and a loss to any one of us, deeply affects us all.

As we consider the events of the past weeks, we need to understand that the Dairy Council has been aware of the possibility of E. coli contamination in milk products for over 10 years. That is why we use only pasteurized milk and why we take just as much care with the eggs and other ingredients in our homemade ice cream as we do with the milk.

In addition, our ice cream vending trailer is one of the cleanest, most modern at the fair. The Barrow County Dairy Council is a nonprofit agency, and all of the proceeds from our ice cream trailer go to local charities. Our families, friends, and neighbors can feel safe while enjoying our ice cream.

*Sincerely,*
*Pat*
*Barrow County Dairy Council president*

Dear Editor,

I am appalled at the lack of concern for the health and safety of the citizens of this county. The county health board should immediately shut down the county fair.

We moved to this community to escape the decay and dangers of the city. We certainly didn't expect to jump out of the frying pan and into the fire. My daughter and I barely walked through the fairgrounds and we both became ill. It is time for the decent people in this community to take a stand and bring this county into the 21st century. This is no longer an agrarian society, and there is no need for the disgusting smells and filthy animals at what could become a nice annual festival.

If the good old boy network here refuses to clean up or cancel the fair, then we should at least make sure that school starts a week before the fair. The truant officer should arrest any student attending the fair during school hours. If students were in school actually learning something instead of playing with filthy animals, there would not have been the tragedies of this past week.

*Respectfully,*
*Claudius Fitzgerald Black*
*concerned citizen*

85

# Letters to the Editor

Dear Editor,

Several people have suggested there is a possibility that Susie Thompson died because she ate a hamburger from our FFA food booth. I want our community to know that there is absolutely no possibility of that rumor being true. We are pretty sure this poor girl didn't even come to the fair. She may have, however, gotten sick at her church camp where she spent most of the fair week.

Besides, our food booth was inspected by the health department and they said we were clean. We also had students from the food service classes at the vocational school helping us cook the hamburgers, and they really know what they are doing. None of our food could have made anybody sick.

*Sincerely,*
*Alex Workman*
*FFA secretary/treasurer*

Dear Editor,

The Barrow County Fair has a 127-year history of displaying the best work of the citizens of this county. Whether it is the needlework or baking skills of some of the finest homemakers in the state, the produce of its best gardeners, the livestock and crops, or the projects of the young people who will be our country's next leaders, the Barrow County Fair is an annual exposition of the best of the best.

This year a few people became ill shortly after attending the fair. While not minimizing the seriousness of their illness, we must not jump to conclusions. Thousands of people who attended the fair did not become ill, and several people who were ill did not attend the fair. A link between the fair and those illnesses has not yet been demonstrated. Until such a link is shown, we would encourage everyone to be patient and trust those who are working hard to solve this problem.

Your county fair board is working closely with our local health department to determine if there is a link between the county fair and the recent outbreak of illness. If such a link is found, you can be certain your fair board will act to insure the health and safety of future fair goers. The investigation by the health department should be completed in the next week or so, and the fair board will make a full and formal statement of their position at that time.

*Sincerely,*
*Stacy Heilman*
*Barrow County Fair Board president*

# MEMO

Date:     Thursday, September 13
From:     Doctor Billman
To:       All Barrow County health inspectors
Re:       Recent apparent E. coli outbreak

I'm saddened and upset to report I just got off the phone with Dr. Goldstein, who informed me that Darryl Harper died early this morning.

I am extremely concerned that we were not able to help Dr. Goldstein make any lifesaving decisions.

I will look forward to getting your complete report later today.

*Dr Billman*

# MEMO

Date:    Thursday, September 13
From:    Doctor Billman
To:    All Barrow County health inspectors
Re:    Recent apparent E. coli outbreak

Thank you for your rapid intervention on behalf of Darryl Harper.

I'm happy to report that he has been transferred to the hospital in Capitol City as you suggested. He has been stabilized and is expected to make at least a partial, if not a full, recovery.

I will look forward to getting your complete report later today.

*Dr. Billma*